FOUNDATIONS OF DIVERSITY

Duncan Smith
in conversation with
Hala Abdelnour

First published March 2018

Duncan Smith
Foundations of Diversity
ISBN 978-0-646-98480-3

Design and layout by Chaun Soh. cssoh@ideasandconcepts.com.au
Printed in Australia

FOUNDATIONS OF DIVERSITY

Similarity and Difference

Majority and Minority

Assumptions and Bias

Inclusion and Exclusion

Power and Privilege

CONTENTS

PREFACE

After nearly 30 years of working in the area of Diversity and Inclusion, I felt it was time to summarize my thinking and approach. Knowing that, like all people, I have a limited perspective, I asked my friend and colleague Hala Abdelnour, someone who I thought would have a different perspective than mine, to interview me about my work. This publication is the result of that conversation.

Since making Diversity and Inclusion a central focus of my professional life in 1989, I have had the opportunity to work in a wide range of settings: industries including banking and finance, infrastructure, consumer products, engineering and technology, legal, professional services, resources, and transportation; governments at the national, state, and local level; sports; and the non profit sector. I have been fortunate to live and/or work in North America, Western Europe, Australia, New Zealand, the Pacific Islands, Asia, and the subcontinent, and have visited Africa and the Caribbean. In every setting I have found both challenges and opportunities in diversity work; and in every setting, I have looked for the fundamentals — an approach that would work in whatever culture or setting I found myself. The common thread, what has kept me going and motivated, has always been the people with whom I've had the opportunity to work — clients, participants in programs, and colleagues. Each consulting engagement, facilitation, workshop, seminar, or conference presentation has been a learning experience – hopefully for the people with whom I have worked, and most definitely for me. I suppose I could call what follows "reflections of a white male diversity practitioner," but I hope there is more to it than just reflections. I have tried to keep the flavour of the conversation Hala and I had on a winter's day outside of Melbourne, Australia, providing you, the reader, with the opportunity to listen in as we explore what to me are the foundations of diversity.

For me, working with diversity is a process of continuous learning, and the conversation that follows is very much a part of that process. I hope you will find it useful.

Duncan Smith
Kallista, Australia
March 2018

ACKNOWLEDGMENTS

Thanks, for helping to shape my thinking, to:

Dr. V. Robert Hayles

R. Roosevelt Thomas, Jr., Taylor Cox, Jr., Marilyn Loden, Amanda Sinclair, Julie O'Mara, Alan Richter

Tom Verghese, Jenny Hutt, Katie Spearritt, Brian D'Netto, Leith Mitchell, Sandy Caspi Sable, Grazia Pecoraro, Anna Carter, Neil Cockroft

Bill Proudman and Michael Welp

Noel Tan, Doreen Teo, Lillian Wang, Andrew Manterfield, Paul Stuart

All the thinkers, practitioners, clients, friends, family, and unexpected strangers who continue to shape my experience with diversity

Special thanks to Hala Abdelnour for having the conversation.

For Carter

INTRODUCTIONS

HALA

Hala: I'm Hala Abdelnour, founding director of Global Echo Consultants, and I'm catching up with my friend and associate Duncan Smith today to discuss diversity and inclusion.

Duncan: Hala Abdelnour – tell me about your name. Does Abdelnour have a meaning?

Hala: It does. Abdelnour is an Arabic name, and it literally translates to slave of the light, but it actually means worshipper of God. It applies to Muslims and Christians across the Middle East and North Africa, and you'll find a lot of men with that name as their first name as well.

Duncan: Abdelnour?

Hala: Yeah, because traditionally, like Abdullah and Abdul — these are different ways of referring to God, and it's like a worshipper of God. Traditionally in the Arab world people would take on their father's name as their second name, and there'd be a broader family name that was an identifier of clan. Your immediate second name was your dad's name. Hence, last names often being men's first names as well.

Duncan: And what about Hala?

Hala: Hala means halo. There was a big hala around the moon last night actually. A kind of ring of light.

DUNCAN

Hala: Okay. Duncan Smith, you even have a white name.

Duncan: I do. Duncan is a Scottish name which from the Scots Gaelic translates as brown warrior or dark-skinned warrior, which obviously I am not.

Hala: A warrior for the dark-skinned people.

Duncan: But then my background is actually not Scottish, it's English; it's actually Norman English on my mother's side, back to people who came across with William the Conqueror, so I guess there's Viking influence further back. My father's side is Swiss/German/Norwegian. Smith of course is a craft name.

Hala: So that's interesting anyway, lineage. That's a big thing these days with all the DNA testing and back to a point you've made previously in our conversations, we are one race. The science is really uncovering that at the moment, so it's nice to keep that in perspective, that actually we all link back to the same parents eventually.

ABOUT THE CONVERSATION

Duncan: I appreciate the opportunity to have this conversation with you. For me it's around 30 years that I've been consciously working in the diversity field, both full time and making it part of other work. It's great to have a chance to reflect on some of my ongoing questions and learnings.

I also look forward to sharing our perspectives given that we are coming at the topic from different backgrounds. To me the most important thing any of us can do to work well with diversity is to bring different backgrounds and perspectives together, and have the conversation.

THE IMPORTANCE OF DIVERSITY WORK

Duncan: The most important thing to me in all of this work is that it's based on making human connections. Are there things that get in the way of our being able to make good connections with other people? Sure, there are all kinds of things that can get in the way. And what helps to make connections? I think ultimately what helps, when I think about diversity and inclusion work... more and more I'm understanding and believing that awareness, consciousness — mindfulness is being used a lot as a term these days — *that* essentially is what's required in order for us to make strong and positive human connections. We need to be aware and conscious — mindful — of ourselves, and how we are responding to other people.

Are there aspects of other people that influence how we're responding? Clearly the answer is yes. That then is what tips me towards an interest in diversity work.

Another reason diversity work is important to me is because my demographic has been controlling the levers of power for a long time, and has created many problems, and that is unsustainable. We all need to figure out how to work effectively with people who are different to ourselves. I'm using 'we' in two senses here: one is the we, the members of the white male demographic that's been in power, need to figure out how to work effectively with people who are not like us; and then the wider we, as in humanity, needs to figure out how to work together better. I'm coming at this work with both of those perspectives in mind. I can't escape my demographic, but does it make sense for people in my demographic to have so much power over the decisions that are being made, relative to our portion of the population? To me, no, it doesn't.

What does make sense is for people who are affected by decisions to be part of the decision making process. In fact, driving the decision making process. One example, here where we're speaking in Australia, is conversations around Aboriginal and Torres Strait Islander people. To me it is absolutely a no-brainer that the people who ought to be making the decisions about indigenous people are indigenous people. It makes absolutely no sense for white people to be making decisions for indigenous people. It makes no sense to me.

Hala: When you're coming from an equitable perspective it doesn't make sense. But when you're coming from the perspective of gaining as much as you can for yourself and those you see as part of you, if somebody else is going to be disadvantaged by your decision, but you're in a position to make that decision, it does make sense that you would make it. If you're not going to be inclusive. If you're not going to create equity.

Duncan: Agreed. Now to me, that's ethically wrong, but that's just my perspective.

Hala: Absolutely, so it's unethical, but it makes sense, because it's power-driven, right?

Duncan: It makes sense, yes. It makes logical sense if you accept that power dynamic as a given, and that replicating that power dynamic makes sense. To me, it does not make sense; it's a recipe for disaster and destruction to hold on to that existing power dynamic. We run a much greater risk, in my opinion, of destroying the entire planet by continuing the way we have been with a relatively small demographic with a limited perspective, and limited decision making options, to be controlling where we're going.

That, to me, is a recipe for destruction. The revolution of having more people around the decision-making table is actually something we have to do for survival. To some extent, the people in my demographic need to, I think, get out of the way, listen, and actively create equity. Which is going to mean having, as a group, less power. I think that's fantastic personally. And I'm sure there are plenty of my cohort who don't.

Hala: Otherwise they would have done it by now.

BACKGROUND IN AND APPROACH TO DIVERSITY WORK

Hala: So what got you started in this work, and how have you approached it?

Duncan: I guess what kicked me into this whole field was looking at global issues and global problems like war and famine and climate change and the arms trade – problems that threaten the survival of the human species.

It seems to me that we need to be able to come together and work together as people, as humanity. How do we do that? What enables us to work together with people who have different backgrounds and different views? How do you get these kind of multi-sector, multi-disciplinary, multi-ethnic, gender, etc. groups of people to come together to actually solve global problems? That's the motivator. The framework of the Foundations of Diversity that we'll be discussing here is what to me helps achieve that coming together and working well together.

Hala: It's quite a big ambition.

Duncan: Yes, I suppose it is. I was listening recently to the wonderful Rosabeth Moss Kanter from Harvard Business School, who said, "You might as well think big because it takes just as much energy and time to think small." She also said, "Act larger than you are." I think of that not in terms of being boastful or swaggering but because there are things going on that are important to think about. At the same time I think it's great and important to work locally. All of this is built on the idea that to be able to work together well we need to focus on the *how* of working together.

To me, organisations are collections of human relationships and the strength of those relationships determines the strength of the organisation. It's that aspect of how we work together that interests me the most.

Hala: I'm really getting an image now of your objective, of this overarching framework. So if the world is a very diverse place, how do we bring all the different people, all the different sectors, all the different organisations together to have a good conversation about solving some of the major world problems or challenges or issues?

Duncan: Like living together in peace so we can sustain and maintain the world that we live in. It seems fundamental that we are all engaged in looking after humanity, but we need to work together to do that.

Hala: Absolutely, and something that comes to mind listening to you is, people need to come together and talk about whatever it is, the environment or climate change or the industrial economy or whatever it is. So who are these people that come together? In this diversity work that you do, who do you bring to the table that isn't usually there?

Duncan: There are a couple of ways to look at that. When I first started doing diversity work we didn't use the word inclusion as much; now we do, which I think is a good thing. It takes me to the first of the foundations we'll be discussing, which is similarity and difference, or 'us and them.' Who is coming together to make decisions? Who is being included? Who is being excluded? And who is doing the including or the excluding?

I know that I'm coming at the whole topic from a particular perspective that's limited, and that I'm not entirely conscious of what the limits of that perspective are. In other words I've got my blind spots, which is one of the reasons we're having this conversation – because I've made the assumption that you might see things or understand the topic in ways that I'm going to be blind to.

So, on the one hand, bringing people to the table in terms of how the diversity field has developed is a focus on people who have been more traditionally in lower power positions. I do want to say at the outset that I'm very aware that I'm coming at this from the perspective of an older, white, straight, physically-abled male, and I realise there's a limit to my perspective. So on the one hand there's been this focus on people who are disenfranchised, not at the table, not having the voice. Then how do we create a more inclusive system to bring those people in? But then who's "we?" Who's doing that bringing in? Do we assume it's people from my demographic? In which case that's where it gets into the whole power and privilege dynamic.

There are things that have developed in the diversity field that I both embrace and question. One is: 'create more diversity around the table in terms of who's having the conversation to be more inclusive of people who have not traditionally had the power.' On the other hand, there is an implicit assumption sometimes that diversity does not include my (straight, white, physically abled, older male) demographic.

Even now as we're speaking [in Australia in 2017], when we look at a lot of the work being done in gender diversity for example, it's being done mostly by and for straight white women. So there's definitely exclusive work going on within the diversity field. I think having a systemic view does mean changing the balance of the demographic of who's at the table and particularly who's in power.

I guess there's a certain level of self-interest in my thinking, but I also want to be at the table. As an executive I interviewed some years ago put it "I don't want to trade one straight jacket for another." Another way I would say it is, if our decision-making structures are a house, let's not completely get rid of the house that's there, but let's expand the house substantially, so that more people, and a greater variety of people, are working together to solve problems.

I'll tell you a little story to illustrate part of what I'm thinking. I was running a session for a law firm a few years ago. We'd been underway for about ten minutes when out of the corner of my eye I saw somebody hovering at the door who then eventually came in and sat down at a seat right in the front. She said to me: "I'm sorry I'm late. I knew I was supposed to be coming to a diversity workshop, and when I looked into the room and saw you, I thought I must be in the wrong place."

So immediately, the assumption is that someone who is white, older, and male doesn't fit within the category of — or have an ability to connect with — diversity. So she left, and then found out that actually she had been to the right room after all, that this was in fact the diversity workshop, and she came back. Most useful to me is that she shared her thoughts – and it's that honest conversation that makes this story a good example of the level of disclosure that I think is critical to the larger diversity conversation.

This story also illustrates for me an example of what I think is an error in thinking. Sometimes we hear the phrase "diverse employees," or "diverse candidates." What does that actually mean? In the U.S. one way of using the term would be to describe, to use an American-ism, 'people of colour.' Again, I have a little bit of an issue with the term, because to me, we all have a colour.

Hala: Absolutely.

Duncan: If I go to a country in Asia or in Africa or somewhere where I'm in the minority in terms of skin colour, who is the person of colour? I think acknowledging everybody's colour is useful[1] and I think it is particularly important for white people to acknowledge whiteness because in white dominated countries we haven't had to.

It's as though in so many areas, white experience and particularly white male experience has been universalized, but most whites and particularly white

---

1   See the wonderful work of Brazilian photographer Angélica Dass, especially her Humanae project. http://www.angelicadass.com/humanae-work-in-progress/

men don't see that it's been universalized. We just accept that it has and we don't actually think about it.

Part of white male culture is that we don't think we have one.[2] We have this oblivion to the dynamics of what it's like to not be in our demographic. We just think, "Oh yeah, well everybody gets a fair chance, and fair opportunities — Australians would say 'a fair go' — and it's all fine and if we treat everyone the same, we're not discriminating against anybody." There's a lot to unpack.

Hala: In the conversation of diversity and inclusion, the power imbalances — the global power imbalance — that's really the elephant in the room isn't it? So, let's take it from the experience of Duncan Smith. Given your demographic, and the limitation of your perspective, how do you get drawn to the conversation? And what do you contribute to the conversation?

Duncan: I think one thing that that draws me to the conversation is becoming conscious of and thinking about the automatic privilege. At the same time understanding that having that systemic privilege doesn't mean that as an individual I feel privileged. So having to wake up to the systemic privilege that I have, when on a day to day basis I might not be experiencing that I have a level of privilege, is something that is one of the challenges.

In my work, one of the areas I'm most interested in exploring is waking up the majority — waking up the power majority — the majority of people in the power positions around that table where decisions are being made — which is my demographic.

---

2 I am indebted to Bill Proudman for his excellent work is this area

So there's that realization that, "Oh I have this privilege. I've been unconscious of it. Now I'm conscious of it."

That changes my perspective on interpersonal dynamics and global dynamics, which are the two things I'm interested in. The other thing that draws me to a conversation is oddly enough being part of the 'right' demographic in terms of being white, male, straight, physically abled, privileged, and being in the corporate system. I had the interesting experience when I was in my last full time corporate job, when I was in my mid 30's, where I felt that "I'm the person that is supposed to be benefiting from this system, but I don't feel like I belong here. Something is not right. I don't feel included as part of this system. I somehow feel different. Not in a way that anyone could see, but experientially there's something going on here that just doesn't feel right to me."

I'm conscious as I say that, that given all the privilege I do have, maybe it comes across as….well, I don't know what it comes across as, but it is my lived experience of not fitting in — a sense of "I don't fit the mould, I don't do corporate politics, I'm not in the money-and-power-grab game." I'm not naturally competitive, rather more relationship oriented, and both emotionally and intellectually driven. Perhaps not the typical straight white male stereotype. And thinking I don't want to be in the stereotype either. So how do I navigate that sense of, "Here's a system I don't really feel part of even though I'm supposed to?" And yet I'm still part of it.

Around this time I went through a two-day diversity program as an employee at the company where I was working – Digital Equipment Corporation – and discovered biases and prejudices that I was carrying around internally, mostly based around race and gender, that I didn't know I had. So that was a big wake up moment for me to say, "I'm carrying around stuff I wasn't aware of, and it's affecting the way I'm able to work with people from different racial backgrounds, with women and men."

At the same time, I was doing a master's degree in organisational behaviour and adult learning, studying with among others the great organizational development guru Chris Argyris, who did a lot of work on what I would call ways of having conversations about the undiscussable — how do you talk about the stuff that is going on in terms of interpersonal dynamics – particularly in the workplace – that no one's talking about, and that's having a huge impact on how people work together? I also studied cross-racial counselling with Dr. Chester Pierce of Harvard Medical School, who looked at racism as a public health issue. And then there's this diversity piece. So putting these threads together, here are ways to have the conversations we're not having, specifically about race, about gender, about culture, about age, about disability, about flexibility, about power.

So those multiple elements all came together at the same time, and I thought, "That's what I want to do when I grow up!" And I was extraordinarily fortunate to find a mentor at Digital, the wonderful Robert Hayles, who gave me my first opportunities to have some of these conversations – rather unskilfully on my part I might add – and whose example of balancing head, hand, and heart in diversity work continues to inspire me.

So I seem to have both global and quite personal motivations for trying to navigate this field of diversity.

Hala: Okay. So here you are and you've been doing it since 1989.

Duncan: Yes.

Hala: Acknowledging that length of time and the growth that might have happened for you over that time in terms of new revelations and insights, where are you right now in that space? How do you reconcile being in that white male demographic but also doing this work? What is it that you're bringing into this space? How has your work been moulded? What is the gem that you put on the table in this discussion?

Duncan: Honestly, if there is a gem – and I don't know that it is one – it would be the five Foundations of Diversity, which is how I structure my thinking when I'm looking at a situation that involves diversity and inclusion. Are we paying attention to all of these? To me, they're the foundations, they're the basics, and a lot of them fall into the simple-but-not-easy category.

Reflecting over the past 30 years or so, I would say that the field here in Australia has gone from not a whole lot, to more, with a long way to go. I keep in touch with colleagues in the U.S. and around the world, so I'm conscious as much as I can be of what's happening in the diversity field globally, and would say similarly that there has been a lot of growth and, if we look back, some very good progress, and there is much more to do.

One thing I notice is a general trend, not just in the diversity field, to look for the next 'new' thing. I do think that if we're going to work well with diversity, that these five foundations we'll be discussing are essential, and that as in many things it's important to go back to make sure that we've got the foundations solid before we go on to the next new thing.

For example, over the last several years in Australia, unconscious bias has been a hot topic in the diversity field. I think that's fine, and, in terms of my foundations framework unconscious bias is part of one half of one of the five dimensions — so less than one tenth of the things that really we need to be having the conversation about in order to do diversity work well.

So I think if I bring anything it's that sense of, "Okay, these are things that in my experience working across countries, across cultures, whether it's corporate, government, or non-profit, with different aspects of diversity, focusing on these foundations works." So I'm interested in being able to share them.

THE FOUNDATIONS

Hala: Could you talk about what the Foundations of Diversity framework is?

Duncan: Sure. There are five areas that to me are the foundations of doing this kind of work, and I guess over the years working in different settings, in different countries, and with different aspects of diversity, I've been looking for a simple way to describe, "what are the things that we need to make sure we're paying attention to, if we want to do this work well and do it effectively?" I came up with these five that I call Foundations of Diversity.

First of all, SIMILARITY and DIFFERENCE, or what I like to call 'us and them.'

Then the whole idea of MAJORITY and MINORITY and the dynamics between larger and smaller groups of people.

Next, what are the ASSUMPTIONS that are made, and the BIASES that are carried, consciously and unconsciously, about and between different types of people?

Then there is INCLUSION and EXCLUSION — what happens as a result of having a mix of people in terms of who's included who's excluded?

Finally, the whole area of POWER and PRIVILEGE — what kinds of power are relevant in this situation? Who has privilege, and what kind?

I think all of these need to be looked at together to really get your head around what's happening in terms of diversity. My view all along has been, we're dealing with diversity all the time. The question is, how?

FOUNDATION ONE: SIMILARITY AND DIFFERENCE

So we start with similarity and difference – 'us' and 'them'. If we're doing diversity work, who's us and who's them — what are the differences, and the similarities, that we're choosing to work with? I think it's essential that both the us and the them need to be taken into account.

I grew up in a very segregated culture in the white suburbs of Boston, USA. One of the implicit messages I got growing up was that there were parts of Boston that 'we didn't go to.' It was never specifically stated why we, didn't go there, and the "we" was never defined. At the time, I simply accepted this, unquestioning. It was just that there are parts of town that we don't go to. If I were to ask why don't we go there, the answer would be that it was dangerous. End of discussion.

Years later looking back, I realized that those places were predominantly black areas, and more working class or low income areas that my parents considered dangerous, so therefore we didn't go there. By extension — again this was never discussed openly – the implicit message was that the people who live in those areas are dangerous, or are dangerous to us. So here's an us-and-them, that was undiscussed and largely undiscussable. Of course, I was growing up with the white, suburban privilege that we didn't need to discuss it, because everybody was like us — with the exception that the part of town I grew up in, and the high school I went to, were majority Jewish. So I was actually in a gentile, Christian minority in a predominantly Jewish environment. But really, as everyone was white and middle class, it wasn't a big issue. It was a difference we could deal with, if you will.

A more current example is diversity work in Australia which for the private sector is focused a lot around gender, and specifically focused on increasing the representation of women, particularly in executive and decision-making levels. So 'us and them' is men and women, and a lot of the focus is men focusing on 'them', (women), and programmes for women, and not looking at themselves.

One of the things I'm very conscious of is that I don't know what it's like to be a woman in a male-dominated system, or male-dominated environment. On one level, I will never completely understand it, and I will never 'get it', because I can't really put myself in that position. But of course there are also dynamics of us (women), looking at them, (men), so it's a bidirectional system that needs to be worked with.

So we need to be very clear about what we mean by us and them, similarity and difference. The book "Us and Them"[3] looks at some of the significant similarities and differences between people over history, and where the divisions have been. There are categories that existed in the past that don't even exist now, that we don't even know about, that were considered hugely important at the time. So what's relevant now in our culture, in our organisation, in our community? What is it that we need to look at? So the first foundation requires us to get very clear about that, and to locate ourselves within that system.

---

3 Berreby, David, Us and Them: Understanding Your Tribal Mind, Little, Brown 2005

FOUNDATION TWO: MAJORITY AND MINORITY

Once we have decided on the similarity and difference that is relevant to us, or that we want to work with, then there's going to be the question of the numbers. Is there more of one type of person and fewer of another? More of us and fewer of them, or the other way around? There are things we know about the dynamics of majority and minority, and in terms of the foundations of working with diversity, that's a set of dynamics we need to work with. We certainly know that the minority notices majority - minority dynamics more easily. So when we're in the majority we tend not to notice; we can be oblivious to it, which of course has a privilege attached to it. When you're in the majority, you have to work harder to wake yourself up to the fact that that's where you are, because it's easy to kind of fall asleep and just think everything is "normal." It's also important to keep in mind the 30 percent rule – that you need at least 30% of whatever the minority is to change the norms of the way a group functions. So for example, adding one woman to a previously all male group will change the dynamics of behaviour in the group, but it will not change the dominant norms.

To me it's important and helpful to do this work without putting a value judgment on good or bad in terms of majority-minority, but to just notice it, and locate ourselves within either the majority or the minority because that will influence the perspective we're bringing to the work. So we need to locate where we are, who's the us and them? Where am I in terms of majority-minority, and what's relevant about that? I often think that diversity is not so much about those other people who are different to ourselves, and more about our responses to those others – it's less about them, and more about how I'm reacting to them. We need to be aware of what we're thinking, and what we're feeling. If we automatically assume that the minority is 'good' and the majority is 'bad', we set up an antagonistic, exclusionary dynamic that quickly becomes us against them (or them against us depending on which group you're in). I was at a diversity conference in Sydney, Australia in the mid-1990's at which one of the speakers was Thabo Mbeki, who at the time was Vice-President of South Africa. He asked the audience to consider that apartheid was a strategy for managing diversity – which brought a gasp to the room. While needless to say he was not condoning apartheid, he was effectively asking the audience to temporarily reduce their emotional response, and look at the facts of the situation – a majority/minority dynamic (in which in this case the power rested in the minority), and a strategy with a consistent internal logic – albeit one with catastrophic consequences. So we need to identify the majority and minority, locate ourselves within that system, and understand both the dynamics and the impacts.

FOUNDATION THREE: ASSUMPTIONS AND BIAS

The third foundation is looking at assumptions and bias. Once I've decided who is the other, and who is the us, what assumptions do I make about that other person because of that aspect of diversity, whether it's skin colour, gender, or culture, or whatever it is? What assumptions do I make about my own group? What stereotypes do I carry around about my own group, as well as the other? This is an area that I think requires some more detail.

When we meet someone we make assumptions. The question is why do we do this? One way to understand this is to recognize that the human brain has limited capacity to process information. According to some researchers our brain is surrounded with up to 11 million pieces of information at any one time, but can only process 40 to 50 pieces of information at any one time. So there's a big gap between the amount of information we have to deal with and the amount of information we can process. How do we manage this? We take shortcuts.

In my work with groups I often illustrate this process by picking up a pen, holding it up in front of the group and asking them 'what is this?' It usually takes a split second before someone says "pen." I then ask "If you have never seen this particular object before, how did you know it was a pen?" I go on to suggest that if they think about the pieces of information they are taking in, they would include shape, colour, size, position in the room or context it came from…. but they just 'knew' that it was a pen. The question is, how? Usually someone comes up with an answer that relates to pattern recognition. And this is exactly correct. They've seen other things like this — maybe not this exact object, but when I ask the question "what is this," their brain evaluates the available information and then looks for a pattern — looks for a similar piece of information or combination of pieces of information filed away in the brain. So basically what the person has done is to think, "hmmm…here is an object. What shape is it? What colour is it? What size is it? Where did you pick it up from? That reminds me of something…. I've seen things similar to that before, and they were all pens, so I'll say 'pen.'" So that's the process that the brain goes through in order to simply answer the question. And, we go through that process without even being aware of it — we go through it unconsciously. So our brain takes shortcuts and this is an essential mechanism for our being able to function.

We go through this process with pens and other objects, and we also go through it with people. When we meet someone for the first time there's a massive amount of data that is presented to us. I've heard neuroscience research that suggests what we notice most quickly about another person is skin colour —in less than 100 milliseconds – and that we notice a difference in skin colour more quickly than we notice a similarity. What we notice next most quickly is gender – in less than 150 milliseconds. Rounding out the top 5 according to some research are age, facial expression, and visible disability. There are of course many other things we notice about people, and this relates to the foundation of similarity and difference – who's like me and who's not like me.

When I'm working with groups outside of the USA, I often ask the following question. "When I first started talking to the group, you heard an American accent. So, what you know about Americans? What are Americans like?" Sometimes I will preface the question by inviting the group specifically to not be politically correct. I find in some countries, particularly Australia, the groups are more than happy to say what they think about Americans. Responses typically include, loud, (always in the top two or three), confident, opinionated, brash, gun loving, think they rule the world, patriotic, religious, overweight, love fast food, and so on. Sometimes, the list includes items like friendly, open, and other positives, but typically, as is normal with stereotyping, the majority of responses are negative. One of my favourites is "often wrong, but never in doubt." And by the way these have been quite consistent over the 25 years or so I've been asking the question – not related to current political events.

The point of the exercise is not so much to consider the specific information, but to notice the process and how easy it was to come up with the information. The data that we receive through our senses: what we see, hear, touch, taste, smell – are filtered through our experience, through our educational background, through ways we have been socialized, through environments we have been in. And so based on this filtered information, we make assumptions. Because of the speed at which our brain is able to process, most of our assumptions are unconscious. Just as with the pen, we tend not to take the time to stop and think through what assumptions we are making about a particular person at that particular time. But our assumptions add up to our perception of reality. So to use my workshop example, I will say to the group: "you 'know' what Americans are like. If I had a different accent, let's say an English accent, or a German accent, or an Australian accent, or an Indian accent, or a Singaporean accent – and was using exactly the same words — you would have a different set of filters, and make a different set of assumptions."

Our assumptions – our perception of reality – drive our behaviour; our behaviour has consequences, which come back to us in the form of new data. And so the cycle continues. Our job, then, is not to stop making assumptions – we can't. What we can do is to notice, in certain situations, what assumptions we are making about other people, and to consider in what situations it would be important or useful for us to notice, recognize, investigate, and perhaps challenge our assumptions.

Understanding the mechanism of assumptions is quite important. Then after we've made assumptions, we have bias, which is the preference. I like to use bias in more of an engineering sense, that we can have a positive or negative bias. Here's this difference, here are these assumptions that I'm making based on that difference. Using the example of the assumption that Americans are loud, is that something I like, or not? That's where the bias comes in. I might be drawn to loud people, because I am one, or because I just happen to like them. Or I might not. So, does my assumption trigger a positive or a negative bias?

Hala:　　I'm interested in your ideas around some of those biases. What are the biases we need to be talking about, uncovering, or be mindful of?

Duncan:　When we talk about biases, first of all, I need to think what aspect of diversity is it that we're biased about?

Here you and I are having this conversation, so we can say, "We have an age difference, a gender difference, a culture difference, a skin colour difference." I'm guessing that we probably have some personality differences too, so if we did something like the Myers-Briggs Type Indicator the results would come out to be a little bit different. So what's relevant here and what do we focus on?

Sometimes, we can make an assumption about what is going to be an important difference, and I think that that then goes back to what aspects of my identity are relevant to me, what am I bringing to the conversation, what's important to me, and what might be important to you? I'll share a story. I reckon by the way that stories are very useful in these conversations, and in D&I work in general...

Hala: Oh, absolutely.

Duncan: I was doing some work for a large multinational company as part of a global faculty around inclusive leadership. I was in London for a faculty conference and one of the other faculty members was a woman from African-Caribbean background who was born and lived in London. One night, three of us were having dinner and I was interested in what the racial dynamics were in the UK at that time.

I had lived in England in the 1970s, so I had some sense of what it was like for me to live there and I knew that the population had changed fairly dramatically over the years, and had become a lot more multicultural/multiracial. Now it's 2013, and I was curious.

Plus, I grew up in the U.S. where race is one of the big diversity topics. I was trying to figure out how to ask the question because I didn't know this person particularly well. So I'm being fairly clumsy, trying to find out what the racial dynamic is like in the U.K. She's looking at me, and she said, "What do you want to know?" And I finally said, "Well, what's it like to be black in the UK at the moment?"

Her response was, "Why do you ask?" And I'm thinking, okay, in my mind England is a dominantly white culture, white English is part of my cultural background and she's black and so it would seem to me obvious that this was going to be a diversity issue that was relevant.

She just looked at me and said, "I live in Brixton; basically everybody's black. I don't really think about my skin colour much. Then she said "so what's interesting to me Duncan, is why are you thinking about my skin colour?" And I didn't actually have an immediate answer for that except that I had made an assumption that here was an us-and-them issue that was going to be relevant for her.

She was saying, "That (skin colour) is actually not my big diversity dynamic. That's not a big issue for me." I made an assumption about what the us and them was going to be for her. She turned it around to ask, why was it an issue for me? She was not saying that skin colour is not an important diversity issue - the other person we were having dinner with by the way was a mixed race German/African-American guy who had grown up in Germany and who had yet another different perspective.

This conversation was both useful learning and a great (as in positive) challenge to me to say, "Why am I thinking about that; why did I make the assumption that here's a diversity issue?" I guess it was an example of a few things, one of which was the importance of determining what is the us and them that's having the biggest impact? What do we want to work with? Who's 'we'? If we're trying to navigate a diversity dynamic, what is that dynamic? What assumptions are we making about what dynamic is important, and what are my biases about that?

Fast forward to today, going into many organisations in Australia, when you say "diversity", what's the automatic thing that springs to mind? For most people it's gender, which is actually code for women. Then why is that an issue? Who is it an issue for? Certainly for women. Is gender an issue for men? Most men would say, "No, it's not really an issue for me," so therefore it's seen as a women's issue.

I would argue that it's actually the dynamics between women and men that that need to be worked with if you're going to work effectively with gender. It's stepping back to say, what are we actually talking about here? This is why I struggle when I hear the term 'diverse candidates'. What does that mean? Does it mean people who haven't traditionally been in a particular role? I would say diversity is all of us. How do we get from us and them to a wider us without losing the richness that difference brings to the human experience? There just within that first foundation, there's a lot of ground I think to sort through. And as usual, working with diversity raises more questions than it provides answers.

Hala: I think that was a really good story and it's just making me think about some of the things you're saying like who's 'we'? Who's having the conversation?

This is a question that comes up quite often in conversations that I've had, in terms of when we talk about racism, and people are often talking about the disadvantage they experience. Whether they're people of colour, or gender, or whatever. Anyone who's not representative of the dominant few really. Then... let's stick to racism for now... you'll talk about whites and non whites, and then you can highlight that within every society, and every culture, and among and between groups there are prejudices, and biases.

There are two things there. The first one is there is a theory out there that if you're not in a dominant majority you can't be racist. That kind of brings us to a definition of racism. Which we may not want to get into right now. Those sorts of ideologies are out there. I guess it's about exercising power over others on the basis of race. I can have racism, biases, but I can't exercise power over others because I don't represent the dominant power cohort.

Duncan: Well I would say two things that are slightly contradictory. One is — and it's a bit of a platitude — that there is only one race, the human race. Which is actually something I believe. Then there are differences within that. Which I personally think is a good thing. At the same time I would say, we are all racist in the sense that we make assumptions about people, and we have biases about people based on what is called race. Which is in fact skin colour, and facial structure, hair type, and other characteristics. I think we all do that.

Hala: Absolutely, yes.

Duncan: That's where you perfectly captured how on the one
          hand these five foundations are distinct, and the other
          hand you can't separate them. As you said, we have
          racial differences, and we all make judgements based
          on those characteristics. Then what? Well then the
          majority-minority, the inclusion, the exclusion. What
          are the assumptions? What are the biases? Who's got
          the power? Who's got the privilege? So I think with
          this framework it's important to unpack each one
          while recognising that on one level you can't separate
          them - that you need to do all five at the same time.

FOUNDATION FOUR: INCLUSION AND EXCLUSION

Duncan: So we've got similarity and difference, we've got a majority and minority, there are assumptions being made, there are biases being held in multiple directions. Then we think about inclusion and exclusion. There's going to be a sense of who is included and who is excluded. When we look at inclusion, it's also important to consider that I might think I'm being inclusive, but do you feel included? If you don't, then it's not working. How do I know whether you're feeling included or feeling excluded? How do we look at inclusion and exclusion? How do they work? What does it look like? How does it happen?

Hala: I guess what really comes up for me in that, going back to the idea of the decision making table, is the relevance of whose table it is. If we're just bringing people to the table, at the moment it is a white man's table. You could bring all the people to that table, but it's reliant on the white man agreeing to host. I'm just thinking about the gender conversation, and how old it is in the West. Yet, despite all the changes men could take all the power away from women tomorrow. There's enough legislative power for men to do that. It's the same with any company in the corporate world, or in the government sector, or the public space.

There's no shift in the ownership of power, and therefore — I'm going to play devil's advocate — I'm going to be radical here and say, there's been no change at all just because people are having a conversation. Martin Luther King had an amazing conversation, and made some changes, but still the black movement in America has a long way to go, 50 to 60 years on. What do you say? I'm not a white man, but I'm also not the most disadvantaged person statistically. An indigenous black single mother is the most disadvantaged person in this world statistically.

Is that good enough for her, for us to just keep having a conversation? Because politicians and business leaders know very well that you could waste a lot of time having a conversation, and people feel like something's happening, while you carry on doing what it is you're doing and your position of power actually isn't being challenged. There's a real danger in that.

Duncan: There is, and it's a great point. Looking from my perspective — which is probably fairly closely inside that power structure, even if I don't feel like personally I really fit, but compared to an indigenous black single mother I am very much in it — do I see changes? I would say yes I do. I see changes that are quite slow. I think one of the things that we're doing is to shift the fundamental power of the patriarchy, which has been dominant for how many...

Hala: Five thousand, six thousand years?

Duncan: Let's call it five thousand or six thousand that's fine. On one level if I look at shifting that power, that's part of an us-and-them diversity project, and definitely an inclusion project. I'd put a timeline on that of probably another couple of hundred years. To be able to shift something that's been entrenched for 5,000 or 6,000 years I don't think we're going to do it in 50 or 100. It's going to be a couple of hundred, maybe two hundred, three hundred years of sustained effort to make that happen. Am I optimistic? Yes, I am optimistic, but then it's not going to ultimately affect me I suppose.

I find it's very easy to get quite discouraged in this field. One way that I become less discouraged or more encouraged, is to look back. I think — have things changed in the last 25 years, in the last 50 years? Yes. Are they where we want them to be? No, absolutely not. Who's we? I guess anyone who is looking for a more equitable division and sharing of the power and more inclusive decision making. Are we there yet? Absolutely not. Are we moving in the right direction? I think so. It's easier for me to be optimistic than it would be if I was the indigenous black single mother. I do know that, but it's still worth fighting for I think.

FOUNDATION FIVE: POWER AND PRIVILEGE

The last foundation, which I think often gets left out of the diversity discourse in the corporate world, is around power and privilege. Who has power and who has privilege? Certainly there's been a lot written about and discussed about male privilege and white privilege, and then there's the challenge of systemic privilege, and the relationship between systemic or structural privilege and an individual experience of privilege.

One of my favourite reminders is a story I heard more than 20 years ago now, about a senior white male executive going through a diversity program, and based on what he learned he started using the phrase the 'privilege of oblivion.'

That means I have the privilege to be oblivious to issues that are affecting people who are not like me. The example that this man used was listening to some of the women in this program that he was on talking about their safety concerns, about having to leave the building after dark and walk across a parking lot that was not well-lit, and that they felt unsafe. This male executive — who statistically is probably going to be on the large side, because most chief executives in the US are substantially taller than the average population of men — said he realised that he had never thought about his own personal safety when he walked across a parking lot at night. It would never have occurred to him to think about that. That was the privilege of oblivion that woke him up. And so I think waking up the people in power who have the privilege so they can see the privilege they have is a critical part of this work. What's the impact of that privilege on the people who have it, and on the people who don't?

Those are the five foundations that I think are essential to being able to work effectively with diversity, both to create more diversity and to enable diverse groups of people to make decisions in an inclusive and equitable fashion.

Hala: There is a lot to unpack and I'm actually going to go straight to something more complex. You've touched on power and privilege, you've touched on white privilege, and male privilege. Interestingly, in the context of majority and minority the majority of the world's population is not white.

Duncan: Correct.

Hala: So majority doesn't equate to power necessarily. You've talked about this person's reaction thinking she was in the wrong workshop in your law firm story. You've explained your demographic. I think you took out privilege from your description but privilege is there as well.

Duncan: Absolutely.

Hala: I think that was a really good story and it's just making me think about some of the things you're saying like who's 'we', who's having the conversation, and on whose table? You haven't specifically said this but whose space are you inviting people into? It's usually the people who hold the power that are even able to invite the people into this space.

Then if that's the case they're maintaining power in that space. It's like in sports when you play in your home ground, you're more likely to win. If we're talking about the tribal elements of our brains that are playing a role in this, then what I'm wondering is when people who are different to each other but don't represent the positions of power in the current world, which is white male, straight, middle class....

Duncan: At least in the Anglo European world.

Hala: Well, no, worldwide.

Duncan: I'm looking at China or India for example.

Hala: But you as a white male walking through India have privilege and would be treated like you're superior. White privilege dominates the world, and male privilege dominates the world, so you carry that with you no matter where you go even if you're in a minority. I'm wondering about what happens with a group of people who don't represent that but are different to each other. If that woman in London who said to you 'why is my skin colour an issue for you?' - if she was having that conversation with others, and this is sort of a question that we can't really answer right now, but I'm wondering if those assumptions are brought to the table then? My question is, you're representing the most privileged cohort of humanity that you can be in right now. How do you balance that? Because I see that conversation about skin colour was a learning lesson for you. What can't you get away from in your own self, in your own biases, or what can you do to actually create balance and equality of power in the conversations when you come to the conversation with greater power?

Duncan: The real answer is I don't know. The best guess that I've been able to come up with so far is to try to work out what helps. One thing that helps is knowing and acknowledging my own identity group or groups or demographics. That is one of the things I've learned along the way, thanks to some wonderful work done by a group of people in the U.S. — Bill Proudman and Michael Welp and others — around white male culture.

Part of that white male culture is not seeing ourselves as an identity group – or you could say that a distinctive aspect of white male culture is that we don't think we have one. That's a big hurdle.

I had an experience at a diversity conference in the US back in the 90's; I was in a workshop and we were doing pairs work with someone who was racially different to ourselves. I was partnered with an African-American woman from the Army who was in uniform, and so there were a few differences right there. I remember at the beginning of the conversation she said to me, "Duncan, What's it like to be white?" I had to be honest and say that I hadn't thought about it before. Suddenly I'm having to think about that where normally I don't – that's the privilege of oblivion.

To me, what is important to bring to that conversation is first of all as much clarity as you can muster about your own identity group. Once I see myself as part of a distinct identity group — I've got whiteness, I've got maleness, I've got all these other attributes — that gives me a particular perspective that's limited. I might not know entirely how it's limited but if I know it is limited then I'm saying, "Okay, I'm actually wanting to come at this conversation from a standpoint of equality, knowing that my perspective is limited."

Now, I'm going to have some difficulty in getting past the privilege that I don't see. It's my responsibility to do that, but I actually need other people — I need conversations with people who have a different perspective to be able to see my limits.

One of my master's degree subjects was on cross-racial counselling, taught by Dr. Chester Pierce from Harvard Medical School, a highly distinguished African-American professor who looked at racism as a public health issue.

There were about 50 people in the class, mostly what we call in the States people of colour, and more women than men. I was one of about two white men in the class. This was one of my first lessons in recognising that racism is not just something that white people have, that there was significant bias, discrimination, and prejudice between people of colour on dimensions that I would have never considered or been aware of. That experience is one of the things that's made me think that we all have a limited perspective.

By the way the lesson has been repeated. One example is looking at bias based on skin colour in India between lighter and darker skinned people. So I think that bias, discrimination, and prejudice are not just things that white people or white males have, but because of the privilege, people in my demographic have expressed it more and brought the positional power that we have based on demographics into the equation. We're able to act based on our biases and that has a negative impact on people who don't have the same level of power. However, if you take the white male out of the equation, is there still a bias? Absolutely.

So, I can't get away from my demographic but can we have global conversations? What is the us and them? Because there are going to be similarity and difference issues everywhere. I mean look in India, look in Africa, look in China. There are all kinds of power dynamics — again you could apply this framework of the five foundations to different aspects of diversity. Take the white man out of the equation and I think it still works.

That said, this white male demographic is what I was born into, so I have that perspective. Also, I do think, for me, waking up the majority is one of the critical aspects of my work.

Hala: I actually think now we're getting to the crux of the conversation of how do you bring everyone to the table to discuss the world's problems. Well, let's say, we share the space, and we go to different tables at different times. There's uncovering the biases within the layers of society.

Where I was going with that is that with power comes great responsibility. With power and privilege comes the responsibility to act, and you've highlighted a lot of that already in talking about yourself. With not having power you can be let off the hook in a way. You could say I'm disadvantaged, and I miss out on opportunities. But if you are, no one's shining a spotlight on you really to uncover your own assumptions and biases, because you're not exercising them greatly against anybody else.

Going back to your vision, and the objective of people coming together to solve the world's problems, you can ask the question that if white people cease to be in power tomorrow, would it look any different? Is it a white people problem, or is it just a domination and power problem? I think we both agree.

Duncan: I don't think it's just a white people problem, but that's easy for me to say because I'm white. I do think in the scenario you suggested, if we take the white people out of the power positions and put in a different group, is it going to be the same dynamic? I think so.

Hala: It would be a different dynamic, but would that group exercise or misuse their power and privilege? I think there are enough examples in the world of people misusing power all the time, in microcosms, and then on the macro level of the world. At the macro level right now you could expand it out and say, white male privilege is the most dominant, but if tomorrow that was replaced with somebody else, sure it might look different, but would the misuse of power still exist? We could assume that it probably would.

Duncan: The only place that I'm not sure about, and would like to see how it would work out, would be that if the power structure was dominated by women.

Hala: It's funny I was thinking the same thing.

Duncan: I don't know that it would be necessarily different. It might be. I don't know. I would say looking around the world if you did the kind of racial and cultural replacement to get whites out and put in a different culture, different race, would we still have the same kind of dynamics? I would say if it was male dominated probably yes. If it was female dominated, or preferably kind of equal, from a belief that the benefit of diversity is in the mixture, and a mix that's being done on a basis of equality and equity, maybe that would be different.

Hala: Well none of us have seen....

Duncan: Few of us have societies dominated by women, so we don't know. At a tribal level, at a village level in some cultures yes, but I don't know enough about that.

Hala: No, and it's still functioning within a world that's male dominated, and so they're limited. It would really have to be a whole world that's female dominated to see the differences. I would presume that it would be very different, then just because it's different there's the question of, would it be better or not?

          These are questions we can't actually answer, because we don't have that, but what this conversation is about, what your work appears to be about to me, what I'm hearing is about bringing the different people into spaces of decision making. It's a lot about decision making isn't it actually?

Duncan: It is.

Hala: With an equality of power within that space.

Duncan: Yes.

APPLYING THE FOUNDATIONS

Hala: Tell me more about the work you do with organisations. How do you work with organisations to implement this kind of framework, and what kind of outcomes do you see, or do you work towards?

Duncan: What I'm working towards is trying to create more inclusive cultures where the power is more widely distributed through a more diverse group of decision makers. First of all, how do you get more diversity around that decision making table? As you said before, whose table is it anyway? I think potentially the ownership of the table may change over time, but in order for the ownership of the table to change we've got to get more people around the table, so that we can negotiate whose table it is. It's actually everybody's table — that's the goal. I would say that a lot of my work up until now has been about how do we create and bring more diversity to that decision making table?

To be able to do that, you need to have people who are already at that table, who are interested in making the changes. So what's motivating them to do that? The easy answer is that it's either great vision, or great pain.

There are people in power positions who I think genuinely want to see more diversity, who believe that in order to solve the problems that we've got globally, or even just within an organization, we need as many perspectives, and as many approaches and minds as we can possibly get. So we need to break out of the limits of the perspective that we've been using for the last several hundred years. We're not going to solve global problems using the approach that we have up until now, so we need to change that. And to change the approach we need to get more people around the table who have different viewpoints. Helping to facilitate getting more diversity around the table has been the bulk of my work so far. There are some people out there in power positions who do want to see that. There are others who probably haven't thought about it. And there are still others who will actively resist doing it. I think it's important to work with the people who are already leaning in that direction. That's the vision part.

The pain part is organisations where people are seeing conflict, they're seeing difficulty. They're trying to bring people who are different to be able to work together, and they're struggling to do that. Or they are organisations that have realized — this will show a very strong bias on my part — that really at the end of the day, an organisation is only as effective as the strength of the working relationships between the people in it. If you work on the relationships, you will get the outcomes, because it's the people who are actually doing things anyway, as opposed to focusing on the task, and keeping the people dynamic as something I don't need to think about, because if we just work on the task people will sort themselves out.

I have a strong bias to working on the people side, the *how* we do things, rather than specifically *what* we do.

Bringing that to bear on diversity, then what are the problems we're trying to solve? That's the emerging side of the work for me. Yes, there's creating more diversity around the table, but then working with the table as a system — that's where I get increasingly excited. Are we where we want to be with diversity? No. Are we moving in that direction? Yes. So let's start to get some of those voices who are at the table, working together better. The excitement now for me is how do we help that happen?

Hala: Yes, absolutely. You've talked about globalisation and working across countries, working across sectors, across organisations. Again, I think you've alluded to this subtly in what you've said so far, about working with the table, and the power of the table. What do you bring to that? How do you use yourself to leverage better decisions?

Duncan: What I try to do is to help the people around the table — in the decision making group — to be able to work more effectively together. A lot of that is helping the group to develop their skills in noticing and understanding the aspects of difference that might get in the way of being able to work well together, and developing the skills in working across those differences, whether it's a team, a group, an organisation, or multiple organizations or countries.

Hala: Tell me more about that. What does that look like? If I were a fly on the wall in a workshop Duncan Smith is running, what is it that I'm noticing? What's the vibe, what's the energy? What are you actually working on with the group?

Duncan: Workshops are one setting. Another setting would be coaching a group, coaching a team – being a facilitator to help the group work better. I'm generically what would be known as a process consultant. My assumption is that the answers are already within the system, and that my job is to help bring those answers out, to enable the people in the system to work well together, and to be able to generate solutions themselves. I'm not the sort of consultant that comes in to say, "Here's the answer." I'm the sort that comes in with the questions and the facilitation, but also the experience in what it is that helps people to work together.

To me, what helps, is to be able to notice and acknowledge the inter-personal dynamics, to have a language for describing those dynamics, and for noticing how people are relating to each other.

So, what I'm working on with the group is, how are people interacting in the group? Are there dynamics of similarity and difference, of majority and minority, of assumptions and bias, of inclusion and exclusion, power and privilege going on in the group? Yes there are, as there are in every group. How do we unpack those so we become as skilful in how we work together, as we are in what we're trying to achieve? My focus is on the how. So it could be through a workshop, through education, or facilitation of group process. What happens in the group, if you were a fly on the wall, depends a lot on the nature of the engagement and how long the intervention is. Whether it's group facilitation or coaching, or a workshop setting, one of the things you'd notice is that it's very much built around the interactions between people in the group.

If you have sufficient time, you're working with what's happening in the group in real time. That's the ideal for me – it becomes more a facilitated conversation and coaching. For example, when I'm working with a board of directors or an executive team as a process consultant or coach, I'm feeding back to them how they are interacting with each other, helping them to navigate issues of difference if one perspective is dominating, helping them notice and work with both mainstream and marginal roles and voices as a system. It's helping the group to see those dynamics, and then to develop the capacity to navigate more equitable and more useful ways of interacting and making decisions. So it's skilling people up to notice the *how* through coaching, process consultation, action learning, being present with the group, drawing out issues and concerns, and building on opportunities to increase people's capacity to work well together.

How we work together is something we don't tend to be taught about much, particularly if you've come up through an organisation, as an executive. A lot of our learning along the way is more about what we do rather than how we do it – especially in terms of working well with others, management, and leadership. We may learn the theory, but often we don't get the practice. So my work is to address that gap, whether through a workshop, seminar, or symposium, or through facilitation or coaching of a group or individuals.

Hala: Yes, but you're there with an agenda, right? I mean you're there to drive a certain outcome.

Duncan: Yes.

Hala: It's driven by a belief that diversity is the better way to go, otherwise you wouldn't be doing this work, right?

Duncan: Yes. It's also driven by the belief that diversity is inevitable.

Hala: Okay, I like that better.

Hala: Share a success story with us.

Duncan: Success story? The success story to me is that we're continuing to talk about it. I would say that for me, as much as it can be frustratingly slow as a strategy, or as an approach, that the most important thing we can do in terms of diversity and inclusion, is to keep having the conversations. If we're going to create those decision making groups and bodies, to bring in more diversity, to create an inclusive environment, and an equitable environment in which to solve the world's problems together, then to get there what we need to be doing is having these conversations about these five foundations.

          Again, it may seem simplistic, but I think that these foundations are topics that up until relatively recently we have not been having open conversations about. We're not used to having the conversation, so we're not comfortable having the conversation. Let me stop here and ask who's "we?" It's probably an indication of my white male privilege that if I choose to I can get along without having these conversations.

          In any case, I think both to create greater diversity around the table and to build our capacity to make better decisions, we need to be having the conversations. I see my career so far as very much like planting seeds, and it's hard to know sometimes which seeds are taking root and which aren't. Having worked in this area for nearly 30 years I do see that a lot has changed in that time. More and more people are having more conversations about topics related to diversity and inclusion. Globally, there's certainly a lot of talk and activity, so I'm fundamentally optimistic.

Again to me there are two critical aspects to the work. There's creating more diversity around the table, and then there's getting that table to function well, able to come up with effective decision making, and implement solutions that will take care of the problems. So there's diversity in and of itself as one issue, and then working with it as another.

I would say most of my work so far has been to try to get more diversity around the various tables. Honestly I don't know what impact I've had. I've consciously focused most of my energy on the private sector, because I think that there is so much power — financial power, social power, and political power — in the private sector that if we can create more diversity and shift thinking there, that's a leverage point to create influence globally. I know people who work more in the government, or community sectors or academia, which is great, and I do work in those sectors myself. We need all of it.

RESISTANCE AND CHALLENGES

Hala: I imagine you've come across people who are more resistant to change. I imagine you've worked with those groups. What have been some of your biggest challenges in this work?

Duncan: Honestly, I think that by far the biggest challenge is my own resistance to change. I don't do this work because it's easy or comfortable. Nor do I do it because I think I'm inherently good at it. I do it because I believe it's necessary. What can I do, as an individual person, to try to help bring to life this vision of a more equitable world, and more equitable interactions between people in it? How can I make that happen? The biggest barrier to me is myself. I think that's probably true for all of us – and I'm conscious that given my demographic and the power and the privilege that goes with that, that's just my perspective. I'm trying to find ways that I can open to new ways of doing things while acknowledging that I've got my own interest and survival at stake as well.

Hala: Yes, of course.

Duncan: That's the biggest thing. I guess it reveals a bias that I think what we all need to do in this space, is to be very clear about our own challenges, our own biases, our own assumptions. I've got to start with myself. It's a bit like when I do work across cultures, whatever culture I'm operating in – the host or home culture – that's the one to start with, not the other cultures who are different, but the culture that we're in. If I'm working in Australia, I'll start with Australian culture, if I'm working in the US, with US culture, or if I'm working in Papua New Guinea, with PNG culture. You start with that culture to understand who are we, because that's going to help us understand how we are responding to something or someone who's different.

Hala: So that's quite insightful. I imagine that would help you quite a bit in delivering the work you do, to be so reflective about your own barriers to change.

Duncan: It means I always have something to do, because there are always barriers there. But I also think that, in another way, I can only help and support people to look at and work with their barriers, to the extent that I've looked at and worked with my own. Once you've seen them, and you think okay I'd like to get past that, and how can I do that, that's what I think I can bring — that ability to say, here are some things that help.

So, we help people find a way to look at their own barriers, and then provide tools to work with them. That brings me back to those foundations of diversity. The foundations are the things to reflect on, to have the conversations about, and then to actively work with in terms of group dynamics, organisational dynamics and decision making. Again, it's not as much about those other people who are different as it is about how I'm responding. It starts there. I think for all of us. But, that's just my assumption. It definitely starts there for people in my demographic.

THE FOUNDATIONS IN PRACTICE

Hala: What I'm thinking about in listening to you is that idea — you touched on it earlier — the privilege of oblivion. That idea that you can't actually see privilege if you have it. I'm wondering if someone from a place of less privilege ... I'm reflecting on myself actually, in being a diversity consultant but where my challenge is different. My challenge is sometimes not being too reactionary, or too radical in my approach because I'm talking about personal experience. I might be talking to people who hold power and privilege, whether they're male or female, if they're white. Of course with the male there's the gender element as well.

So there's a lived experience that I bring with me. I don't bring everybody's experience who's in a position of less privilege to the room. But I feel I connect to that more easily, just because I've experienced some level of lack of privilege. Listening to you I don't know that I operate from working on my own barriers to change, as much as 'how do I let go of power and privilege?' It's quite different from my perspective. I'm actually thinking this is a strength for you, in that if we're talking about working with executives and senior managers in organisations, then you're largely going to be working with white people, particularly in Australia and America.

Duncan: Well the Anglo diaspora, — the UK, US, Canada, Australia, New Zealand...

Hala: So the Anglophonic world.

Duncan: Yes, and in Europe too, to some extent, the executive leader level is mostly white and it's mostly male.

Hala: Right. So there's an element that you bring into the room in that you actually can relate, and you can present the material from a position of similarity. You can really reflect on the work you've done on yourself, and apply that.

Duncan: Yes, and I get how threatening diversity can be. Honestly I think for a lot of people in power, white males predominantly, the whole topic of diversity can be scary. Now, most white men are not going to say, "Oh, I find this topic scary." But it's under there, and I get it, because sometimes it's scary for me. Yet, we've got to do it anyway. Obviously I can't speak on behalf of all white men, because we're all different, but there is that systemic component. As you said, can you bring every experience of exclusion or disadvantage to your work? No, but you can bring a lot more than I can.

I did a program recently for a group of emerging leaders within refugee and migrant communities in Australia, so new communities. There were people in the room from multiple communities, 20 different countries represented, and I was the only white person in the room. So I'm the only one that's not living with the level of exclusion experienced by everyone else in the room: the negative impacts of other people having more privilege, or being judged by the colour of my skin. Here I am working with a group of people who just get it — they get it better than I do, because they're living it all the time. Do I have anything to offer a group like that? Based on my experience using this framework of the foundations of diversity to help people acknowledge the issues and enhance their ability to have the conversation, and work with the issues, the answer is yes.

Another example was working in Papua New Guinea, a place where I'd never been, again being the only white person in the room, and asking does this approach, this framework, does it work here? I came away with the answer that yes, it does. What's influencing that assessment? Again, I'm the only white person in the room, but what's the legacy of privilege and power in Papua New Guinea post-colonialism? I'm the outside expert, and I've got an American accent to boot, which gives me even more credibility in this case. *I* think the system or the approach that I brought in worked for the people there. Did it actually work? Or am I looking for evidence that it was working and they're telling me that it's working, and that's it valuable, and at the same time there's the power dynamic, not to mention my own confirmation bias that's going to have me looking for the answer I want to find.

So possibly we can't know for sure, but I think all we can do is give it our best effort.

As you were speaking, I was reminded of something I read recently from an organisation called Men Advocating Real Change, MARC. It was an article about how to be an ally as a man, particularly as a white man — how to be an ally in diversity work with people who are not white men — in American terms, women, people of colour, women of colour particularly.[4] The author had asked some of his colleagues and friends who were women, people of colour, and women of colour. What came back was that the experience of those people looking at a white man, someone like me, that it was a constant experience of "Can I trust you? I'm checking you out all the time, and I'm watching what you do, I'm listening to what you say. I'm noticing who you spend time with, how you respond to situations, there's a constant wondering whether I can trust you."

Something you said earlier reminded me that, again, I need to keep in mind the limits of my perspective. For me, the opportunity to work with and spend time with people like the leaders from the migrant and refugee communities, local people in Papua New Guinea, or if I'm in Asia, or wherever I'm in the minority, that to me is an extraordinary privilege. Now if I can actually help other people like me to realise the huge benefits that we get from listening to and learning from other perspectives, if I can do that, then hopefully that is starting to shift the dial a little bit and create more of that openness.

Hala: Do you think that trust, that question of trust, applies in all cases where the person who is the expert is different to the group?

Duncan: I think there's always a dynamic of 'can I trust you?', to some extent. Maybe I'm going to trust you more if I see you as an expert, but I'm still checking you out. But

---

4 *When Partnering Across Difference, Men Must Bridge The Incredulity Gap* by Jim Morris with Robin Gerald, http://onthemarc.org/blogs/22/481#.Wlv2mBhh2Rt

I don't know, if I'm in that power position. Take the whole post-colonialism dynamic. My background is the colonists, so I don't actually know what it's like to be on the other side.

Hala: But you feel that trust when you walk into a white organisation, where your client is a white male? Then do you feel that you're automatically trusted?

Duncan: Actually no, I don't if I'm coming in to talk about diversity. At best, there's curiosity. Let's put it this way: if I'm working with a group of people, if I'm running a workshop, or I'm giving a talk, and I'm raising issues about us and them, and minority-majority dynamics and issues of trust, and issues of power and privilege, the heads that are nodding, the people who are with me on the topic, are predominantly women and people in a racial or cultural minority because they're living it every day. The white men are more willing to listen because of what I look like, but I've got to work at earning that trust, because the topic is unfamiliar: for some they don't get it, or don't want to get it, or are actively or passively resistant to the change that's implicit in the work that I'm doing, because on some level it's threatening to them.

Yes, I get the automatic privilege of being able to walk in and I will get a sort of a fair hearing because of what I look like.

Hala: I think that's what I'm talking about.

Duncan: That's a big privilege, yes.

Hala: I certainly feel the lack of trust because of who I am, if the audience is…

Duncan: If you walk into a white male boardroom, they're going at you, and on some level thinking, consciously or unconsciously, "Oh, she's different." I walk in wearing a suit, and the unconscious or conscious thinking is, "Oh, okay he's one of us."

Hala: That's right, exactly. But you're not going to get that in Papua New Guinea, they're not going to look at you and say, "He's one of us." You represent power, but you don't represent one of them. That kind of trust isn't there.

Duncan: Correct.

Hala: That comfort with the other.

Duncan: Yes.

Hala: When you're aiming to work across cultures and across countries, across sectors, what kind of work do you have to do? Or what does that look like then? Because if that applies everywhere, how do we, as a global society, get beyond that?

Duncan: Yes, how do any of us generate that trust?

          I think one thing that's important is to acknowledge very sincerely — and to be able to acknowledge it sincerely you need to believe it — that I don't know what it's like to be you. Whatever the 'you' is. Along with that, then do I know what it's like to be me? That's pretty critical, and again what is the us and them difference, what are the identity aspects that we're working with? In my case, do I know what it's like to be white? Do I know what it's like to be male? Do I know what it's like to be the age that I am? Do I know what it's like to be a parent? Sure, on one level I know these things, but do I understand them in a way that I can express to myself and others, and do I understand the impact of my demographic on myself and others? So, it's starting with that self-reflective piece.

I think it's also critical to be able to then have an equitable dialogue. Because I don't know what it's like to be you, where do I start? Well I can start by finding out why would you be willing to tell me what it's like to be you? Why are we having the conversation? For me, we're having the conversation because we want to be able to work well together. And in order to work well together we need to know about each other. When I don't know what it's like to be you, I could be quite interested, and I might be a bit frightened. I might be a bit defensive because of all kinds of dynamics and assumptions that I might be making about how you are seeing me. So we're dealing with things that are typically unspoken — the dynamics between us, right here, right now. What do I do with that? How do we talk about that?

That again is where I come back to the importance of having the conversation. If that's enough to get us working well together, great. Then if we can maintain that conversation about how we're working together while we're doing whatever it is that we're doing, then *that's* great. We need to be able to keep this conversation going to be able to be effective in doing our work together. That's my bias anyway.

Hala: Absolutely. As you said, diversity is inevitable currently in the way the world is moving. People are more and more finding themselves having to work with people who are culturally different, who are religiously different, who are gender different, who are ability different, who are sexuality different. That raises this dynamic you were talking about, that underlying stuff between us. If I don't know you, and I don't trust you, that triggers my primal brain, and there can be a fear there.

Duncan: Exactly.

Hala: So are you facilitating change by addressing people's fears?

Duncan: Yes, and, I think there's more than the fears. The fears can be one aspect of what we're working with. I think there can also be great positives and rewards in working with difference and diversity. We're motivated both by what disturbs us and by what attracts us. We need to have both; I need to see that if I work with my fears I'm actually going to get to a place that's really positive, and is going to have great outcomes. I think because I've had that lived experience of a diverse, inclusive, trusting, high-performing, fun environment and workplace, that motivates me to keep working to understand how to replicate that. Because it doesn't happen by itself. That is then another motivator for doing the work.

Hala: Could you paint a picture of that environment for me? Could you describe a time that you observed this?

Duncan: Sure. I think of my own experience of being in a team, back at Digital Equipment Corporation in the 1980s. I'll acknowledge that the team was all white, but beyond that, it was diverse in terms of gender, age, sexuality, personality, and disability.

The leader of that group intentionally brought together a lot of diversity. She didn't actually use the word 'diversity' or 'inclusion' but she created a very inclusive group where everyone was encouraged to be themselves — to 'bring your whole self to work.' That team was the most high performing group I'd ever been in, in terms of how things were being measured, in terms of what we did, and it was also the most fun place I'd ever worked.

It was that connection between performance and the enjoyment of being in the team that really encouraged me to think about 'how do we do this?' It was that balance between getting the diversity in the team, and working effectively with that diversity by managing and attending to the interactions between people who were different, all with a clear goal of focusing on what we were trying to achieve. It was that balance between the how and the what. What I've noticed in most of my career is that the balance is tipped towards what we do and away from how we do it. I think we need to get the balance back to focus more on the how. So then diversity becomes not something as a goal in itself, it's a goal for specific purposes, because groups of people who are diverse, if they work well together, work so much better and achieve so much more, than groups of people who are similar.

Do I see it when I facilitate a decision-making meeting or a conversation, or in a workshop? My experience is that people will report afterwards that they are seeing things differently, and noticing things they hadn't noticed before. They're having conversations they hadn't had before that are leading to stronger, more effective working relationships and better outcomes. I asked the CEO of a company I had been working with for several years about the return on their investment in diversity and inclusion work – had it done anything? He said, "Absolutely, it's very clear that this has been very worthwhile." I asked how he noticed that, and he said, "Well what I notice is that the conversations around the company are different. People are behaving towards each other in a different way. It feels different. The culture has changed."

Now here's a very numerically driven CEO who is saying, "Although I could point to things like changes in cost of recruitment and lower turnover, and higher productivity, and while there are all sorts of things I actually can put numbers on, what I notice most powerfully is what it feels like." That to me was the success. Can you put numbers on this work? Sure you can, and I'm quite interested in the whole measurement aspect of diversity. But to me the numbers are a lag indicator - a result of being able to have the conversations and get the human interactions working effectively.

Hala: Absolutely. That's certainly backed by the research as well in terms of the higher productivity, the higher profit rates, and more efficiency, and more innovation and creativity costing…

Duncan: There's a big element of trust involved in whether you are actually going to engage in this work. Then you need to trust that it is going to lead to an improvement, and is going to deliver dividends that you might not see immediately, that you might struggle to measure in the way you traditionally measure things. Does it work? I'm convinced that it does.

THE LIMITS OF PERSPECTIVES

Duncan: What have I missed?

Hala: What have you missed?

Duncan: I'm wondering if there's anything further to discuss? Of course every conversation will touch on different things, but I'm wondering what am I completely oblivious to that we haven't touched on yet? Not to put you on the spot…it's as though I'm asking you to speak on behalf of all people who are not white and male, which of course you can't do, any more than I can speak on behalf of all white men. I suppose I can on one level, but on another level we're all individuals…

Hala: If you want to get technical about it, you can only ever speak on your own behalf.

Duncan: Exactly.

Hala: You can speculate, you can represent ideas, you can allude to an experience of being part of a group. You can have similar or shared experiences of the world that you can talk about, but even when you talk about it, it's your version of events.

Duncan: Yes.

Hala: Absolutely. I find that I'm well aware of that. I travelled around the world for two years, and I know that whenever I was in a non-white country, I was from Lebanon, I wasn't from Australia. When I was in a white country, I was from Australia. I was playing those two identities to my advantage. Because, at the end of the day we live in a world where you need to understand and work with the power dynamics where you are. Sometimes I needed to shed power so that it didn't work against me. For example in most of South-East Asia they thought they were better off than Lebanon, which was great, because I didn't get the sudden walking dollar sign treatment.

Duncan: So being able to navigate in those situations, where you're dealing with multiple us-and-them dynamics, and different aspects of identity, then you have the capacity and the fluidity to figure out how to navigate this?

Hala: Absolutely.

Duncan: As you said before, and as I wrote about 20 years ago now[5], we're all dealing with diversity all the time anyway. So then the question becomes how are we dealing with it, how consciously, what's my response to these differences, and what do I want to be doing with this? It's really about becoming more aware, and more conscious of something that's happening anyway. Then being able to use that consciousness to our collective advantage.

---

5 *The Business Case for Diversity, Monash Mt Eliza Business Review 1998*

Hala: Absolutely. For me it's also not seeing diversity as a linear progression towards greater power and privilege, but rather layers that are intertwined. We see that these days, there are some measures of privilege, like these exercises you can do where you end up with the white person being not necessarily the most privileged if they're female and disabled, or gay, or whatever.

    You see people ending up scattered, based on whatever privilege points they have. So for me, navigating myself through the world was navigating through these layers that overlap with each other sometimes. I found a place of privilege within a space of less privilege. That was what was going to work for me.

Duncan: Listening to you helps me realize that at least for the foreseeable future, there will be a range of power and privilege. There will be some people who have more power and privilege, and some people who have less. Still we can have the goal of creating greater equity, and maybe reducing the size of the vertical relationship in the power dynamic. I guess having that goal reflects a bias I have coming from a nominally egalitarian culture. And also vastly increasing the diversity of who has the power and privilege, and creating a more equitable global society. With any luck that will help us survive for a little while longer as a human species.

Hala: Yes, and possibly help other species. I'm thinking of the corporate sector and the mining sector, if they were to listen to the communities that don't want to be displaced, and that care about the earth that is being dug up, then those species that live on that land will be listened to as well, indirectly.

Duncan: Yes.

Hala: There are around the world various guardians and custodians of land, and of space, and of anything that comes with that, and we're missing out at the moment by not listening to that.

Duncan: And is it important for us to care about that? In my opinion, absolutely yes. Again, that's why the listening, the coming together, the bringing together greater diversity to solve both the problems we have, and the problems we are creating, is so important. I think humanity will always be a work in progress. The more parts of humanity we can bring together to work together, the better both our present and our future will be. I think this is critical.

Hala: That makes me think about how we measure wealth. So really to see the greater benefit of this, you have to measure wealth by more than just money, more than economic wealth.

Duncan: Absolutely.

Hala: Again, these are indirect gains that you don't really get to experience or see until you allow yourself in that space. To truly value it I think you have to live it.

Duncan: Yes - and for many people who are used to focusing primarily on material gains, that very concept is threatening.

Hala: Definitely.

Duncan: I think that one thing we need to do with diversity

work is to deeply understand the level of threat, and the fear that some people feel around this whole idea of diversity and looking at things in a different way. Even the idea of wealth being defined differently is going to be scary and threatening for some people. For me it's important to be able to work with that fear, and work with the people who feel threatened, to help them navigate the change. It's particularly tricky when the people who feel threatened have a lot of power and could derail the process really easily. Working with those people in a skilful way is critical.

Thinking about what you said before, there's a fine line for someone like me. How much am I colluding with the system because of my position of privilege and how much am I moving people towards change? I know that I'm not always going to get it right, and that there will be, I think, in an ongoing way, many people who are not in the white male demographic, and who will look at me and think, "You don't get it, and you never will get it." I guess what I would say is that I agree. And so then what do I do? Well I think I work for the changes that I believe in, as well as I can, knowing that I don't get it from another perspective entirely — but that's not a reason to stop trying.

Hala: Having this conversation with you, I certainly have thought about white people in the diversity space. What I've noticed from the conversation, to frame it in your terms, is what do I not have? What about me? If I'm going to look at you, why not look at myself? What I've noticed is that I don't relate to the white male the way you would, because I'm not one. That's what I can't bring to the table. If I want to have a conversation, I need to try to relate as best as I can. What you bring to the table is representing the group that possibly needs this kind of work the most, in terms of equity and in terms of reaching these goals. I do believe everybody brings a gift to a space, and everybody brings a challenge to a space. Again, the beauty of diversity is that if we can work together towards these things, use each other's gifts, support each other's challenges….

Duncan: So hopefully our respective gifts and challenges balance each other out.

Hala: Balance out, and I think create a less threatening approach.

Duncan: Yes.

Hala: Absolutely. I think this work for me is about reducing threat, not creating threat.

CHANGING THE SYSTEM

Duncan: If I'm looking to create changes in a particular system that's dominated by a group of people, if those people feel threatened, then it's more difficult to make that change. I do understand there have been arguments for revolution throughout history, although if we consider recent history of five or six thousand years of patriarchy, what are we missing in terms of the perspective of the history that we get? There's a level at which I understand the attraction of revolution, and people being more driven by, "You know what, you people – the people in power — just don't get it. I'm angry. Get out of here and let somebody else do it."

I don't think that approach ultimately is going to work in the sense that, from my limited understanding of history, the result will be just another power structure, and another us and them. I go back to what that executive I worked with once said about not just trading one straightjacket for another. How do we actually shift the whole way we're approaching this problem solving? It's possible that the people I find difficult to work with are the ones I most need to work with. But I need first to understand why is that difficult for me? I need to get my own work done first, so that I can actually have the conversation with the people who right now, I find it more difficult to have the conversations with.

Diversity is great when I'm thinking about the differences that you and I bring to this conversation, see great things to explore, things I'm interested in and intrigued by, and am not having a fear based reaction to you in the conversation. There are people out there with whom I do have that more fear based reaction, and that's the edge to work with. It's easy to talk about, harder to do. I come back to the idea that diversity is simple but not easy. That's why this framework of the Foundations of Diversity is somewhat simplistic. Yet I wouldn't begin to think that it's easy to navigate any of those dimensions, let alone all five of them at the same time. And, I think that's exactly what we need to do.

ABOUT THE AUTHORS

Duncan Smith helps people work together, better. Over his career he has become a trusted advisor to his clients, working with organizations, teams, and individuals in the United States, Europe, Australia, and the Asia-Pacific region. Duncan's work includes leadership and executive team development, designing and implementing culturally appropriate diversity and inclusion solutions for multinational organizations, and facilitating critical conversations to overcome barriers in the areas of unconscious bias, gender and cultural diversity.

Duncan is particularly known for his ability to help clients with issues including developing leadership capability, responding to globalization, increasing productivity, attracting and retaining top talent, enhancing creativity, innovation, and problem solving capabilities, and improving service delivery. With a strong interest in the development of an equitable global society, Duncan focuses his work on the ways our national, organizational, and personal cultures affect how we work together, so that we can collectively solve problems and build stronger relationships across lines of difference.

A lover of languages, people and creativity, Hala has lived, travelled and worked in approximately 50 countries. She has participated in event management, sales, teaching and development. Hala is the founder and director of Global Echo Consultants, a change agency focusing on effective strategy, diversity and collaboration; she joined the Diaspora Action Australia Board in 2014 as a member and was elected its Chair in 2016.

Trained in Psychology and Social Work, Hala seeks to share ideas and knowledge that allow people to grow together through their working relationships. She has dedicated her career to working with diverse populations and exploring innovative business practice and effective behaviour change processes.

globalecho.ct@gmail.com   www.globalechoconsultants.com.au